D1020701

Library of Congress Cataloging-in-Publication Data available.

ISBN: 978-0-8118-6825-9

Manufactured in China.
Designed by Jenny Kraemer.
Illustrations by Brenda Brown.
Visit www.worstcasescenarios.com

10 9 8 7 6 5 4 3 2 1

Chronicle Books LLC
680 Second Street
San Francisco, CA 94107
www.chroniclebooks.com

CONTENTS

INTRODUCTION

There's no place in the world that's quite like New York City.

Whatever you want, whatever you're looking to do, New York has it. Whether you want world class cuisine or the world's greatest hot dog, to see masterpieces of art or masterworks of graffiti, to stare at celebrities or the craziest person you've ever seen, you can find them all in the Big Apple.

But it's not a town for the faint of heart, for the panic stricken, for the weak-kneed, or the weak-bladdered. New York can be a cruel and unforgiving place, if you don't know how to survive it. The morning commute alone could be your downfall. Or crossing a street. But staying in your room isn't the answer either—cockroach infestations are everywhere. There's a reason that the song says, "IF" you can make it there you can make it anywhere.

The "IF" is key—making it in New York is by no means guaranteed. Just making it uptown isn't even guaranteed.

That's where this handy little guide comes in. Like its larger *Worst-Case Scenario Survival* handbook predecessors, *The Worst-Case Scenario Pocket Guide: New York City* provides you with the clear, step-by-step answers you need to survive The City's inevitable and unexpected turns for the worse. In addition, you'll find useful charts, lists, and instant visual solutions to help you navigate and survive The City's perils.

Whether you're a first time visitor to New York or a seasoned Manhattanite, don't be caught unprepared. You'll definitely find something in this pocket guide that will help you survive New York. At the very least, it's a great place to hide your credit cards.

—The Authors

New York has always been going to hell
but somehow it never gets there.
—Robert Persig

Chapter 1
Getting Around

TAKING THE "A" TRAIN

HOW TO SWIM ACROSS THE EAST RIVER

1   Strip naked.
Leave on only a belt.

2   Put your clothes in a garbage bag.
Tie the bag closed so air remains. Using eight feet of thick, waterproof rope, tie the garbage bag to your belt. Leave six feet of slack rope between the bag and the belt.

3   Jump into the river.
Holding the bag and slack rope in one hand, run and jump feet first into the river.

4   Swim in a straight line.
Swim the crawl stroke, alternating 50 arm strokes with eyes closed and head submerged with four strokes swimming with

Run and jump feet first into the river.

11. *Getting Around*

your head above water. Locate the nearest
bridge and use it as a reference point.
Each time you bring your head up, refer
to the bridge to ensure you are moving in
a straight line. Scan the horizon in either
direction for waterborne obstacles.

5 Use the garbage bag as a flotation device.
To restore your strength, cling to the bag
with both hands. Hold your head above
the surface and tread water until your arm
strength returns sufficiently to continue
swimming.

6 Emerge from the water in Brooklyn.
If you have emerged in Queens, get back
in the water.

7 Untie the garbage bag from your waist.
Put your clothes back on.

8 Take a shower or bath.
Bathe in clean, fresh water as soon as possible to remove any sediment and pollutants from your skin's surface.

Be Aware

- There are relatively few points on the Manhattan side of the East River where it is possible to dive directly into the water. Before diving, look down; if you see FDR Drive, find another embarkation point.
- The water in the East River is generally clean, though full submersion is not recommended by city authorities. Do not drink the water.
- The ideal time for river swimming is approximately 7:40 A.M., when the river is at high tide.
- Avoid potential hazards including ferry traffic, power boats, empty bottles, oil drums, discarded fishing line, nets, hypodermic needles, and corpses.

NEW YORK CITY DISASTERS

Disaster
King Kong
Godzilla
Stay-Puft Marshmallow Man
Manhattan Sinking into Hudson
Giant Meteorite
Draft Riots in "Five Points" Area
Global-Warming-Fueled Tidal Wave
Alien Mothership Hovering above City
Dr. Octopus

AND THEIR SOLUTIONS

Solution

Chase up Empire State Building; distract with blonde; shoot down from planes

Entangle in Brooklyn Bridge; shoot down with missiles

Cross proton streams, creating protonic reversal

Swim to Jersey; choose to drown

Send tough, handsome men to blow up with A-bomb

Send in Union Army; have naval ships fire cannons into crowd

Huddle in main branch of library; await assistance from Mexico

Send U.S. jet fighters, led personally by the president

Recruit Spider-Man

HOW TO HAIL A TAXICAB

1 Stand "upstream" from other taxi seekers. Position yourself so a cab coming down the street sees you first.

2 Step to the curb.

3 Lean forward with your arm extended at or above shoulder height.

4 Check both directions.
Turn your head rapidly from left to right to watch for a cab and to guard against someone moving in on your territory.

5 Protect your position.
Stare at anyone who approaches. Squint your eyes and shake your head aggressively, while continuing to wave your arm at the street.

Chapter 1: Taking the "A" Train

Lean forward with your arm extended.

6 Signal for all cabs.

Do not limit yourself to cabs with lit domes. An occupied cab may be dropping someone off; an "off-duty" taxi may just be screening potential passengers.

7 Lock in the cab.

Once a driver sees you, nod at him, sealing the contract. Maintain eye contact with the driver and slowly lower your arm from its hailing position.

8 Signal the direction you want to go.

Indicate a U-turn, a turn at the far corner, or that the cab should pull up exactly to the place you are standing.

9 Enter the cab.

Be Aware

- It is illegal for a taxicab driver to ask where you're going before accepting you as a rider, and it is your right not to answer until you are in the taxi and it has pulled away from the curb. A New York City taxi must take you to your requested destination within New York City, Westchester County, Nassau County, or Newark Airport.

- Off-duty cabs, car services, and "gypsy" cabs may pull over in response to your cab-hailing gesture; it is not illegal to ride in a gypsy cab, but you will likely pay more than you would in a licensed city cab.
- The standard tip on a taxi ride is 15 percent.

SIGNS IT'S TIME TO
LEAVE A TAXI

- Taxi stuck in traffic, being passed by strollers, pedi-cabs, pedestrians

- Taxi going 50+ miles above speed limit, up on two wheels

- Taxi being pursued by police or National Guard

- Driver asking you for directions

- Strong odor

- Taxi filling with smoke, flames

- Banging, cries for help coming from trunk

- Driver texting

- Driver vomiting

- Driver drinking out of paper bag

- Driver sobbing, expressing loss of will to carry on

HOW TO ESCAPE A STALLED SUBWAY CAR

1 Alert the authorities of the situation.
Locate the two-way radios at the front
of all train cars. Depress the button. Wait
for the green light to come on, and speak.
Release the button to listen.

2 Move forward to the next car.
Walk to the front of the train (in the direction that the train had been traveling) if
the danger is in your car. Grasp the handle
of the door at the front of the car and pull
it to the right to unhitch. Slide the door
open and step carefully over the coupling
between cars to the door of the next car.
If you cannot see in the darkness of the
tunnel, use a cell phone or other mobile
device to cast illumination on the tracks.

Lie down in the depression between the rails
if the train starts moving behind you.

3 Remain on the train.
Do not get off the train unless you are in immediate danger and have no other option.

4 Exit the train car and climb down from the coupling between cars.
Take off any backpacks or other encumbrances. Shimmy under the metal fencing that links the two cars and step down onto the track bed. Step over the tracks to the platform wall. Avoid stepping on the "third rail," which runs alongside the subway tracks and carries more than 600 volts of electricity. Climb up onto the platform.

5 If you cannot reach the platform, walk alongside the tracks until you reach a benchwall.
Hug the platform edge and move as quickly as possible in the direction the train was traveling. Locate the benchwall, a small

passageway leading off the main tunnel.
Enter the benchwall and await help.

6 If the train begins moving behind you,
lie down.
Find the depression in the concrete between
the rails and lie down. There will be enough
room for the train to pass over you.

Be Aware
- Newer subway cars have call boxes at
  both the front and rear of each car.
- Pull the emergency brake before leaving
  the train car. This will make it impos-
  sible for the train to move, so it cannot
  run you over once you are down on the
  tracks. Do not pull the emergency brake
  unless there is absolutely no other way
  out, as demobilizing the train will com-
  plicate potential MTA rescue efforts.

Worst Subway Lines

Least Reliable	Dirtiest
5	F
4	7
2	J/Z *(tie)*
R	Q
6	V
A/F *(tie)*	D
V	2/G *(tie)*
B	N
Q/D *(tie)*	E/L/M *(tie)*
3	A/C/R/W *(tie)*

INSTANT SOLUTION

RETRIEVING YOUR KEYS FROM A SUBWAY GRATE

Prepare a "fishing line."
Hook keys with bent hanger attached to string.

HOW TO SNEAK PAST A DOORMAN AFTER EVICTION

1 Observe the building from across the street. Wear a hat and stand in the shadows. Try not to look creepy.

2 Wait for the doorman to be distracted. Look for opportunities when the doorman:
- is greeting a steady stream of tenants entering and exiting at once (such as at the beginning of the morning commute).
- is on the street, hailing a cab for a tenant.
- is greeting a parent pushing a baby in a stroller, or a tenant walking a cute puppy.
- is retrieving a package from the package room.

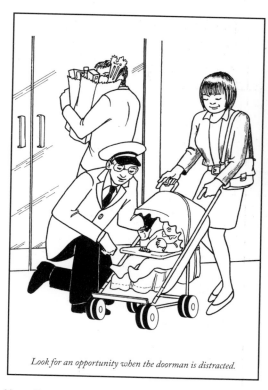

Look for an opportunity when the doorman is distracted.

3 Walk briskly and confidently into the building.
Carry a pile of mail, a small package, or a shopping bag.

4 Go directly to the elevator bank.
Press the "up" button. Keep your back to the reception desk until the elevator doors open.

5 When leaving the building, again wait for an opportune moment.
If you must walk past the doorman in full view, wave heartily and nonchalantly say "Hello."

Boo! York City

Place

Algonquin Hotel *(44th and 6th)*

Bridge Café *(16½ Dover Street)*

Belasco Theater *(44th and 7th)*

Brittany Residence Hall, NYU *(55 East 10th Street)*

The Dakota Hotel *(72nd and Central Park West)*

St. Paul's Chapel *(209 Broadway)*

White Horse Tavern *(567 Hudson Street)*

One if by Land, Two if by Sea *(17 Barrow Street)*

Morris-Jumel Mansion
(175 Jumel Terrace, Washington Heights)

New Amsterdam Theater *(42nd and Broadway)*

Haunted Places in Manhattan

Haunted by

Dorothy Parker and other members of the Algonquin Round Table

Pirates

Theatrical impresario David Belasco

Former students

John Lennon

George Frederick Cooke, beheaded British actor

Dylan Thomas

Aaron Burr

Colonial Era socialites

Ziegfeld girls

HOW TO FREE YOURSELF FROM A DOG WALKER'S LEASH TANGLE

1 Calm the dogs.
Use a deep, authoritative voice and order the dogs to "sit" and "stay." Repeat as necessary.

2 Ask the other dog walker to remain still.
Do not attempt to untangle the leashes at the same time (especially if Step 1 was unsuccessful), as the leashes may become increasingly entangled.

3 Grasp your dog's collar.
Crouch down and reassure your dog that everything is going to be okay. Maintaining your grip on the end of the leash with

Ask the other dog walker to remain still.

your right hand, grab the collar of your dog with your left hand, as close to the scruff of her neck as possible.

4 Drop the leash.
When you have firmly secured your dog by her collar, release the leash from your right hand, letting it drop to the ground. Remind the dogs to be calm.

5 Pick up the leash closer to the collar.
Hold the dog in place with your left hand. Pick up the leash again with your right hand, this time as close as possible to the dog's neck, where you are gripping the collar with your left hand.

6 Reel in the leash.
Gently tug on the leash with your right hand, threading it through the other leash, your dog's legs, the other dog's legs, and the other dog owner's legs.

7 Resume normal leash carry.
Once the leashes are untangled, move your left hand back to the end of the leash.

8 Let go of the collar.
Release your grip on the collar.

9 Resume walk.

Chapter 2
Daily Survival

DO COCKROACHES HAVE ARMS?

HOW TO SURVIVE A COCKROACH INFESTATION

1 Rid your kitchen of any food residue.
Thoroughly scour the kitchen counters, dining table, stovetops, and any other areas where food is prepared or consumed. Remove all food from the kitchen and clean inside all cabinets and drawers. Empty, rinse, and scrub every trash can. Clean the refrigerator inside and out, the underside of the microwave, and the crumb tray of the toaster.

2 Clean the rest of your apartment.
Pull out sofa pillows and vacuum away any crumbs using a crack-and-crevice attachment; roll up all carpets and sweep and mop the floor underneath.

Chapter 2: Do Cockroaches Have Arms?

Eat out instead of cooking in your home.

3   Dry your apartment.

Look for puddles underneath the sink, around the base of the bathtub, and next to the toilet. At each sink, turn on both taps and, as the water is running, examine the base of the faucet, the tap handle, and the underside of the sink. Tighten the joints and recaulk any areas of seepage. Repeat this procedure with the taps in the bath.

4   Eliminate roach hideouts.

Get down on all fours and crawl from room to room, carefully examining each pantry, closet, drawer, and cupboard. Destroy any potential roach hiding places, such as bags stuffed with other bags, piles of old magazines, or cardboard boxes waiting to be recycled. Open old boxes, take out their contents, flatten the cardboard, and remove from your apartment.

5 Place "survey traps" in ten sites around your apartment.

Position "sticky traps" throughout the apartment. Place each trap against a wall or corner, under a sink, or along the baseboards.

6 Monitor the traps.

Carefully note the number of dead roaches in each trap to determine where in your apartment the roaches are most prevalent.

7 Kill the roaches with borax.

Mix 4 parts borax with 2 parts flour and 1 part cocoa powder. Sprinkle liberally in roach-heavy areas of your apartment.

8 Maintain a clean, dry apartment.

After each meal, thoroughly clean the areas where food was cooked and consumed. Store all food in sealed containers. Do all dishes immediately. Take out any garbage and recycling at least once a day. Make sure to immediately clean up any water spills and repair leaky faucets. Whenever possible, eat out instead of cooking in your home; do not bring home leftovers.

9 Convince your neighbors to keep equally clean.

Be Aware
Read the sticky trap instructions carefully, especially if you have pets and/or children.

SIGNS OF A ROACH INFESTATION

Roach droppings	Small clusters of black, ridged pellets measuring one-eighth of an inch.
Gastro-intestinal problems	Potential ailments include diarrhea, vomiting, and dysentery. Caused by organisms transferred from the arms and legs of cockroaches onto food and utensils.
Allergic responses	Symptoms include watery eyes, skin rashes, sneezing, and congested nasal passages. Caused by the presence of roach droppings and molted roach skin in the air.
Cockroach sightings	The most common cockroach in New York is the German cockroach, which is a tan or light brown winged insect, measuring from half an inch to an inch, with two dark streaks down its back. You may find roaches: • in the kitchen, or any area with abundant food • in the bathroom, or anywhere there is standing water • in or near the garbage or recycling

HOW TO ESCAPE A SWARM OF PIGEONS

1 Run in a zigzag pattern.

2 Pull your shirt over your head.
Crouching forward at a 30- to 45-degree angle, reach behind your head with one hand and grab the nape of your shirt. Pull your shirt up over your head. Stretch it far enough forward that it covers your entire scalp and your eyes.

3 Scatter food.
Use your free hand to remove any food from your pockets and bag and throw it in every direction. Employ vigorous flinging motions to draw the attention of the pigeons away from you and towards the food. Toss the food as quickly and as far away as possible.

Chapter 2: Do Cockroaches Have Arms?

Pull your shirt over your head and flap your arms like a falcon.

45. *Daily Survival*

4 Flap your arms like a falcon.

Extend your arms completely and flap them up and down vigorously.

5 Make loud noises.

Jump up and down and clap your hands repeatedly. Bang trash can lids, set off car alarms, scream, or make other loud noises that will scare away the pigeons.

Be Aware

- Pigeons cluster around partially eaten and discarded food, especially starchy items such as soft pretzels and hot dog rolls. Avoid people sitting on park benches distributing handfuls of popcorn, grain, or seeds.

- Pigeons are highly unlikely to peck your neck and eyes, but depending upon the season, may try to claim strands of hair for their nest. Defecation is frequent.

- A pigeon peck is not strong enough to break human skin.

Chapter 2: Do Cockroaches Have Arms?

- The primary health hazards associated with pigeons stem from the three illnesses caused by pigeon droppings: histoplasmosis, cryptococcosis, and psittacosis. All attack the respiratory system and pose the greatest danger to anyone with a compromised immune system.
- If you come into contact with pigeon droppings, wash the affected area immediately and as thoroughly as possible. Be on the lookout for flu-like symptoms over a 14-day period after the initial contact.

INSTANT SOLUTION

STEPPED IN DOG POOP

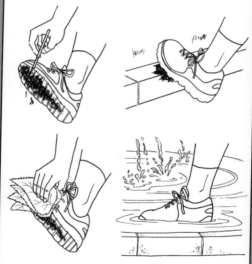

Use a stick to scrape out poop from between the treads of your shoe. Drag sneaker through grass or over edged curb. Dip shoe bottom into park fountain.

HOW TO SURVIVE
A RAT BITE

1 Wait for the rat to let go.
Rat bites typically last only a few seconds, and it is preferable to withstand the pain of the bite than to attempt to fling the rat away, which will create a messier wound.

2 Remove the rat.
If after several seconds the rat has not let go, pinch the upper jaw of the rat with your index finger and thumb and gently pry its incisors out of your flesh. Place the rat on the ground.

3 Staunch the bleeding.
Hold a dry, clean handkerchief or other small piece of cloth against the bite until bleeding subsides, which should only take a few seconds. In the event of persistent bleeding, tear a piece off of your shirt and

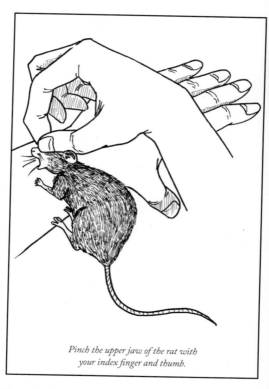

*Pinch the upper jaw of the rat with
your index finger and thumb.*

Chapter 2: Do Cockroaches Have Arms?

tie it tightly around the wound, pulling
the piece of cloth closed.

4 Dress the wound.
Clean the bite mark, and any other parts
of your body that came in contact with the
rat, with soap and water. Flush the soap
fully out of the wound to prevent irritation.

5 Remove jewelry.
Take off any rings or other constricting
jewelry, as swelling of the extremities may
occur.

6 Bandage the wound.
Use a bandage or gauze and adhesive strip,
applied loosely enough so that air can
circulate to the wound.

Be Aware
- Rat-bite fever (streptobacillus monili-
formis) can appear up to ten days after
a bite, even after the initial wound has

healed. Symptoms include back and joint pain, vomiting, headache, fever, and a rash, usually on the hands and feet.

- The upper incisors of rats are approximately four millimeters long and 1.5 millimeters wide. Their lower incisors are seven millimeters long and 1.2 millimeters wide.

- Rabies has never been passed to a human from a rat in the United States. Rats do, however, carry a host of other diseases, including the hanta virus, salmonella, and hepatitis E. They can also carry parasites such as maggots, botflies, lice, and ticks. All of these things are more likely to be passed by skin-to-skin contact with the rat than through a bite.

THINGS TO DO WITH YOUR TRASH DURING A GARBAGE STRIKE

- Dump in public cans on street

- Place in dumpster behind restaurant

- Leave in taxi

- Put in trunk of rented car

- Gift wrap and leave at building entrance

- Put in shopping bag and leave on the downtown local

- Store under roommate's bed

- Make into sculpture, seek grants

- Stand on Brooklyn Bridge, drop onto passing barge

- Sell online

- Compost in Central Park

HOW TO SURVIVE A MUGGING

1 Do not resist.

Remain calm and follow the mugger's instructions. Answer questions slowly with an even tone of voice. Avoid any hints of sarcasm, irony, or aggression. Do not look directly at the mugger's face.

2 Attack vulnerable areas.

If you are certain the mugger means to do you harm, take swift aggressive action.

- Thrust your fingers into the mugger's eyes.
- Hold your hand flat and chop sharply at the mugger's Adam's apple.
- Grab his crotch and squeeze.
- Thrust your knee up into his groin.
- Swiftly sweep your left foot into his right ankle. At the same time, grasp his left elbow and pull sharply downward. As the mugger begins to totter, lunge

Chapter 2: Do Cockroaches Have Arms?

Attack vulnerable areas.

forward into his midsection, pushing
your attacker to the ground.

3 Use an object as a weapon.
Clench a car key between two fingers and
use it to poke or stab. Wield a glass bottle
to use as a bludgeon, or, if broken, as a
knife. Break off a car antennae and use it
as a weapon.

4 Flee.
Run as quickly as possible to the closest
well-lit area, such as a store or a crowded
sidewalk.

Be Aware
Most street criminals want to get what
they can and make a quick getaway. There
is no possession worth losing your life over.
- Do not call attention to any mobile tech-
  nological device you may be carrying.
- Whenever possible, walk in small
  groups and avoid dim, isolated areas.

INSTANT SOLUTION

SURVIVING THE TIMES SQUARE NEW YEAR'S BALL DROP

Do not kiss strangers more than once.
Watch your wallet in your back pocket.

HOW TO SHARE A STUDIO APARTMENT WITH THREE ROOMMATES

⭐ **Put everything in writing.**
Before all roommates move in, create a "roommates contract."

⭐ **Label all possessions.**
Put your name on your food, books, CDs, portable electronic devices, clothing, and pets. Nothing, including food, should be considered "communal property," unless explicitly agreed upon by all roommates in the contract.

⭐ **Utilize feng shui.**
Minimize clutter, decorate with bright

Subdivide the room into several tiny mini-apartments.

colors, and hang numerous mirrors to max-
imize the feeling of openness and harmony.
Store or throw away any possessions that
are unnecessary. As many furniture items as
possible should be designated "multi-use":
futon pulls out into bed, ottoman turns
into night table, bathtub with plank of
wood across it becomes desk.

✪ Subdivide.

Place a bookcase in the middle of the space
to give the illusion of multiple rooms;
repeat several times until the apartment is
divided into several tiny mini-apartments.
Hang framed signs at the entrance to each
"room," with titles such as "Bob's Room,"
"Allison's Room," and "the parlor." Put tape
on the floor to demarcate various territories
and provide directions.

✪ Communicate.

Convene weekly roommate meetings
to maintain an ongoing dialogue. Each

Chapter 2: Do Cockroaches Have Arms?

roommate should keep a notebook to write down things that are bothering him. Share complaints and positive support at the weekly meeting. Encourage all roommates to use "I" statements to express their feelings in a calm, nonconfrontational manner.

ROOMMATES CONTRACT

- A rotating chore schedule for undesirable communal responsibilities: cleaning the toilet, taking out the garbage and recycling. Specify individual responsibilities: doing laundry, walking your dog, washing dishes, watering the plants.

- Financial obligations: who pays for what and in what proportion, including heat/electric/gas, rent, maintenance-related costs, and any shared food.

- A schedule for sharing communal resources: shower, kitchen, TV. If there are not enough beds or sofas for every person to have one, specify who gets to sleep at what times—and rotate.

THAT'S A PRICEY CLOSET

Neighborhood	Studio: 2002
Chelsea	$1,624
East Village	$1,535
Gramercy/Flatiron	$1,710
Midtown East	$1,500
Midtown West	$1,832
Murray Hill	$1,552
Soho/Tribeca	$1,581
Upper East Side	$1,448
Upper West Side	$1,476
Wall Street/Battery Park	$1,862
West Village	$1,710
Manhattan Average	**$1,621**

Average Costs of a Manhattan Studio

Studio: 2007	Percent Increase
$2,189	35%
$1,973	29%
$2,235	31%
$2,105	40%
$2,075	13%
$2,079	34%
$2,448	55%
$1,854	28%
$1,991	35%
$2,258	21%
$2,216	30%
$2,129	**32%**

WHATCHA LOOKIN' AT, PAL?

HOW TO SURVIVE MUSEUM FATIGUE

⭐ Prioritize.
Proceed immediately to the exhibit or
section of the museum that is of most
interest. Then move to other parts of the
museum. Do not wander. Utilize a detailed,
annotated map and have a plan.

⭐ Block out all external stimuli.
Periodically remove audio tour head-
phones. Drop museum maps and exhibit
catalogs. Shut your eyes and cover your
ears with your hands. Hum vigorously
to yourself until you have cleansed your
sensory palate.

⭐ Lie down.
Be completely still and breathe deeply in
and out.

Periodically shut your eyes and
cover your ears with your hands.

67. *Culture and Sights*

⭐ **Drink coffee.**
Slowly consume one or more cups of coffee or other caffeinated beverage in the museum cafeteria. Stare at the table or into your beverage. Do not discuss the contents of the museum. Do not think museum-related thoughts. Sip your beverage.

⭐ **Eat healthy snacks.**

⭐ **Leave the museum.**
Sensory and cultural overload begins after 60 minutes and peaks at 90 minutes. Do not remain at the museum beyond this point.

⭐ **Go shopping.**
Clear your head with a value-free, noncultural activity such as shopping, riding the subway, or sitting in a park.

⭐ **Return to the museum.**
To catch the exhibit you missed, it is safe to return for half an hour after shopping.

LOOK BOTH WAYS

Most Dangerous Intersections for Pedestrians	Average Accidents per Year
East 33rd Street & Park Avenue	156
Utica Avenue & Eastern Parkway	120
Webster Avenue & East Fordham Road	99
Essex Street & Delancey Street	86
7th Avenue & West 34th Street	85
Atlantic Avenue & Nostrand Avenue	84
East 167th Street & Grand Concourse	79
8th Avenue & West 42nd Street	77
63rd Road & Queens Boulevard	72
East 183rd Street & Grand Concourse	71

HOW TO GET INTO AN EXCLUSIVE NIGHTCLUB

1 Wear expensive shoes.

Do not dress sloppily or outlandishly in an attempt to be "unique" or "interesting."

2 Go on a slow night.

Pick a night when fewer people will be trying to get in. In the summer, try a Friday or Saturday night. During all other seasons, go on a Monday, Tuesday, or Wednesday night. Avoid nightclubs during high-profile events such as Fashion Week (twice yearly) and the New York Film Festival (early fall).

3 Travel in a group.

Approach with no more than six people, including at least three women.

Do not give anyone a "high five."

The women should give no indications of being "taken," such as holding hands with the men in the group; holding hands with one another is okay.

4 Remain calm.
Maintain a laid-back, sober attitude while in line. Do not be argumentative with the doorman, the club staff, or with passersby. Do not name-drop or otherwise try to bluff the doorman into thinking you are more important or interesting than you are. Do not attempt to bribe the doorman or bouncer for entry. Do not complain when others arrive and get in while you are waiting. Do not bring a book to read while in line.

5 Be casual when you do get in.
Nod calmly at the doorman as he waves you inside. Do not give anyone a "high five." Do not begin dancing until you are on the dance floor.

Be Aware

To increase your odds of being allowed in on a subsequent visit:

- Don't tell anyone you are from Jersey.
- Order full bottles rather than individual drinks. If there is a price for table service, or for use of a "VIP" area, pay it willingly. Tip at least 35 percent on each round of drinks and food; if possible, calculate the tip without reference to a calculator or wallet-sized tip card.
- If you see celebrities, do not ask for autographs or take photographs. Be polite but not overly flirtatious with the bar staff and cocktail waitresses
- Tip the doorman at least $50 as you exit the club.

WAYS TO FIND AN APARTMENT IN NEW YORK CITY

- Scan online listings

- Hire real-estate agent or broker

- Bribe a building superintendent

- Encourage friends with desirable apartments to join Peace Corps, leave country

- Read newspaper obituary section

- Wander desirable neighborhoods in search of "FOR RENT" signs

- Become *au pair*/personal chef/butler

- Fall in love, move into partner's apartment

- Pretend to fall in love, move into partner's apartment

HOW TO SURVIVE THE CONEY ISLAND HOT DOG EATING CONTEST

1. Stand close to the table.

2. Lean slightly forward.

3. Remove the first hot dog from the bun. Place the bun within immediate reach on the table.

4. Tear the hot dog in half.

5. Shove the two pieces of hot dog, side by side, into your mouth.

6. Chew and swallow.
   While chewing and swallowing, pick up the bun and dunk it in your cup of water.

Culture and Sights

7 Eat the bun.
Insert the entire water-logged bun in your mouth; rapidly chew and swallow it while picking up the next hot dog and breaking it in half.

8 Repeat steps 3 through 7 until time is called.

9 Drink water after every third hot dog.
Drink enough to lubricate your esophagus, allowing the hot dogs to go down smoothly. Do not drink too much, or your stomach will fill up with water.

10 Swallow and open.
At the end of the 12-minute competition, swallow whatever is in your mouth and open to show that it is empty.

BEFORE THE CONTEST ...

★ Expand your stomach.
In the weeks before the competition, drink

Dunk the hot dog bun in water to ease swallowing.

lots of water and eat nonfattening foods like celery, pineapple, and cabbage.

⭐ Do not fast.
Extreme hunger will shrink your stomach and make you a poorer competitor.

⭐ Eat a light breakfast.
On the morning of the competition, eat slightly less than usual. Arrive at the contest hungry but not excessively so.

Be Aware

- Partially eaten hot dogs count towards the total number eaten, and are judged in increments of one-eighth of a hot dog.
- Water refills are provided throughout the competition.
- The winner of the contest is awarded a cash prize of $10,000, as well as a "jewel"-encrusted belt of mustard yellow.
- "Reversal" (vomiting) is an immediate disqualifier.

Instant Solution

Getting Through a Large Approaching Group

Aim for middle. Divide two most vulnerable people.
Do not make eye contact. Do not break stride.

PARADES, RACES, AND OTHER

Event	Timeframe
Lunar New Year Parade and Festival	Chinese New Year (late January or early February)
St. Patrick's Day Parade	March 17
AIDS Walk	Third Sunday in May
Puerto Rican Day Parade	Second Sunday in June
Gay Pride Parade	Third Sunday in June
Village Halloween Parade	Halloween
The New York City Marathon	First Sunday in November
Macy's Thanksgiving Day Parade	Thanksgiving Day
New Year's Eve Ball Drop	December 31

EVENTS THAT SNARL TRAFFIC

Affected Areas

Chinatown (Mott Street; Canal Street; Bayard Street; East Broadway; Worth Street)

Fifth Avenue between 44th and 86th streets; 86th Street between Fifth and First avenues

Central Park

Fifth Avenue between 44th and 86th streets

Fifth Avenue from 52nd Street to Greenwich Village; Christopher Street and surrounding areas

Sixth Avenue from Spring Street to 21st street

Throughout the city; ends in Central Park

Central Park West from 77th Street to Columbus Circle; Broadway from Columbus Circle to Herald Square

Times Square

HOW TO SURVIVE A SAMPLE SALE

1 Arrive early.
Spend the night on the sidewalk outside the sale location to secure a place in line.

2 Bring cash.
Sample sales rarely accept credit cards.

3 Be decisive.
Proceed directly to the racks or tables that hold the items of most interest to you. Take each garment that you like with you as you continue to search.

4 Try the garments on.
Once you have gathered all the clothes you are interested in, try them on. There are no exchanges or returns, so make sure that each item fits. There are no fitting rooms, so change in the aisles.

5 Examine every item carefully.
Check items for damage such as makeup
smudges or perspiration stains.

6 Maintain physical contact with your
selections at all times.

7 Be aggressive.
Follow shoppers who are holding items
you want. Once an item is put down, it is
considered available.

8 Dissuade other shoppers.
Tell someone who is trying on an item
you want, "It's too bad they don't have that
in your size."

9 Avoid over-buying.
Do not become excited by the steep dis-
counts and purchase unnecessary articles.
• If you cannot readily imagine a use for
the outfit, you do not need it.

Change in the aisles.

Chapter 3: Whatcha Lookin' at, Pal?

- Tailoring costs can easily cancel out even the most dramatic savings.

Be Aware

- Wear a layer of form-fitting, color-neutral underclothes. If you are a woman, wear a tank top or camisole and light-colored tights. If you are a man, wear full coverage boxers or boxer-briefs and a tight, white undershirt.
- To find the best deals, wait until later in the day, or the sale's second or third day when the crowds will have dissipated and prices have been further discounted.
- Most items sold at sample sales are overstock or items from a previous season, but some are damaged or have been worn at runway shows
- Sample sales are often held in "found space," so you cannot return; check online and newspaper announcements for more sales.

VARIOUS SUBWAY CHARACTERS AND SOLUTIONS

Ignore	Change Seats	Change Cars
Person keeps talking to self	Person keeps talking to you	Person keeps shouting, intended audience unclear
Person with blaring headphones	Person drumming on seat	Three-piece mariachi band
Panhandler	Person selling bootlegged DVDs out of suitcase	Slow-moving group of teenagers selling something indeterminable
Person holding an ice pack to a wound	Person bleeding from wound	Physical fights, with or without weapons

HOW TO GET INTO THE GOSSIP COLUMNS WITH-OUT KILLING SOMEBODY

BECOME FAMOUS ...

⭐ Inherit extraordinary wealth.

⭐ Become very good at something and rise to the top of your field.
Choose a high-profile profession such as film actor, real-estate developer, or professional athlete. Make surprising and/or bold career decisions that shake up the profession and shock the public. Win multiple awards.

⭐ Become famous-by-proxy.
Enter into a romantic or intimate relationship with a person who is already famous,

even if the relationship only lasts for a brief period. Lavish physical attention upon the already-famous individual in a public or semipublic location. Capture the intimacy on camera. Blog about the encounter, and encourage other bloggers to link to your blog.

ONCE YOU ARE FAMOUS ...

★ Stop doing whatever it is that made you famous.
Focus all your energy on your personal life.

★ Note the locations mentioned in gossip columns and go to those places.
Frequent trendy nightclubs, film festivals, art openings and other major Manhattan social events. Draw attention to yourself by dressing provocatively, drinking heavily, and complaining about the contents of your swag bag.

Date someone famous, if only briefly.

⭐ Frequently enter and exit drug and alcohol rehabilitation programs.

⭐ Frequently begin and end intimate relationships.

⭐ Feud with other famous people.
Make outrageous statements about other celebrities. Deny having made such statements. Retract your denial. Repeat.

OTHER ROUTES ...

⭐ Hire a publicist.
Be prepared to pay as much as $10,000 a month, with no guarantee of results.

⭐ Offer a quid pro quo.
Barter scandalous information about celebrities (they have cheated on a spouse or committed a string of crimes) with gossip columnists in exchange for placing your own name in the column.

INDEX

ACKNOWLEDGMENTS

David Borgenicht would like to thank Sarah O'Brien, Jay Schaefer, Steve Mockus, Brianna Smith, Jenny Kraemer, and Brenda Brown for making this book happen—he'll meet you on the top of the Empire State Building at midnight on Christmas Eve.

Ben H. Winters is deeply grateful to Sarah O'Brien, David Borgenicht, and everyone at Quirk and Chronicle for welcoming him into the delightful Worst-Case universe. He'd also like to thank all the experts for their input, as well as all his friends, friends-of-friends, and total strangers who replied to his weird and random "does anyone know . . ." e-mails. Finally, a word of advice: If you call the Metropolitan Transportation Authority many times, with a lot of really specific questions, people start to get a little suspicious.

ABOUT THE AUTHORS

David Borgenicht is the creator and coauthor of all the books in the Worst-Case Scenario series, and is president and publisher of Quirk Books (www.quirkbooks.com). He visits New York every month, and has only been caught in the subway doors once. He lives in Philadelphia.

Ben H. Winters lives in Brooklyn, where he writes for the theater, hangs out with his little family, and periodically takes the F train to Coney Island to root for the Cyclones. This is Ben's first book, and he's delighted that—just like another great story of New York, Edith Wharton's *The Age of Innocence*—it includes a chapter about a hot dog eating contest.

Brenda Brown is an illustrator and cartoonist whose work has been published in many books and publications, including the Worst-Case Scenario series, *Esquire*, *Reader's Digest*, *USA Weekend*, *21st Century Science & Technology*, the *Saturday Evening Post*, and the *National Enquirer*. Her Web site is www.webtoon.com.

MORE WORST-CASE SCENARIO PRODUCTS

VISIT OUR PARTNERS' WEBSITES FOR MORE WORST-CASE SCENARIO PRODUCTS:

- ✪ Board games
  www.universitygames.com
- ✪ Gadgets
  www.protocoldesign.com
- ✪ Mobile
  www.namcogames.com/WorstCaseScenario
- ✪ Posters and puzzles
  www.aquariusimages.com/wcs.html

For updates, new scenarios, and more, visit:
www.worstcasescenarios.com

To order books visit:
www.chroniclebooks.com/worstcase